Profiles in Greek and Roman Mythology

POSEIDON

Mitchell Lane
PUBLISHERS

P.O. Box 196
Hockessin, Delaware 19707
Visit us on the web: www.mitchelllane.com
Comments? email us: mitchelllane@mitchelllane.com

PROFILES IN GREEK AND ROMAN MYTHOLOGY

Titles in the Series

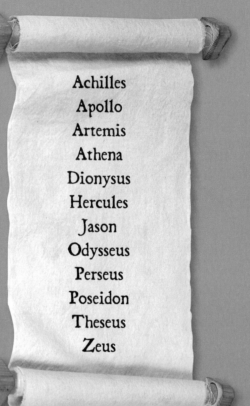

Profiles in Greek and Roman Mythology

POSEIDON

Russell Roberts

Mitchell Lane
PUBLISHERS

P.O. Box 196
Hockessin, Delaware 19707
Visit us on the web: www.mitchelllane.com
Comments? email us: mitchelllane@mitchelllane.com

Printing   1   2   3   4   5   6   7   8   9

Library of Congress Cataloging-in-Publication Data
Roberts, Russell, 1953–
   Poseidon / by Russell Roberts.
       p. cm. — (Profiles in Greek and Roman mythology)
   Includes bibliographical references and index.
   ISBN 978-1-58415-707-6 (library bound)
   1. Poseidon (Greek deity)—Juvenile literature. I. Title.
   BL820.N5R63 2009
   398.20938'01—dc22
                                                                                    2008020917

ABOUT THE AUTHOR: Russell Roberts has written and published nearly 40 books for adults and children on a variety of subjects, including baseball, memory power, business, New Jersey history, and travel. He has written numerous books for Mitchell Lane Publishers, including *Nathaniel Hawthorne*, *Thomas Jefferson*, *Holidays and Celebrations in Colonial America*, *Daniel Boone*, *Athena*, *Zeus*, and *The Lost Continent of Atlantis*. He lives in Bordentown, New Jersey, with his family and a fat, fuzzy, and crafty calico cat named Rusti.

PUBLISHER'S NOTE: This story is based on the author's extensive research, which he believes to be accurate. Documentation of such research is contained on page 45.

The internet sites referenced herein were active as of the publication date. Due to the fleeting nature of some web sites, we cannot guarantee they will all be active when you are reading this book.

To reflect current usage, we have chosen to use the secular era designations BCE ("before the common era") and CE ("of the common era") instead of the traditional designations BC ("before Christ") and AD (*anno Domini*, "in the year of the Lord").

Every effort has been made to locate all copyright holders of material used in this book. If any errors or omissions have occurred, corrections will be made in future editions of this book.

PHOTO CREDITS: p. 6, 15—Carly Peterson; p. 8—Antonio Fantuzzi; p. 12—J. Paul Getty Museum; p. 14 (top)—Hans Andersen; p. 16—Frans Francken II; p. 17—Henry Justice Ford; p. 18 (top)—Bartholomeus Spranger; p. 18 (bottom)—Jacques de Gheyn III; p. 23—Solomon Joseph Solomon; p. 28—Sir Edward Coley Burnes-Jones; p. 31—Pierre Mignard; p. 32—Frederic Leighton; p. 33—SPSG; p. 39—Jacob Jordaens; p. 40—Johann Wilhelm Bauer; p. 41—Gustave Doré; p. 42—Adam Lambert-Sigisbert.

TABLE OF CONTENTS

Profiles in Greek and Roman Mythology

Neptune, the Roman equivalent to the Greek sea god Poseidon, is the central figure in the Trevi Fountain in Rome. The Romans adopted many of the ancient Greek deities and stories as their own.

CHAPTER 1

The Contest

It was a contest the likes of which no mortal had ever seen before. A god and a goddess—he with a powerful trident, she with a spear—stood poised above the Acropolis, the highest point in the city, prepared to strike the ground and bring forth a magnificent gift for the citizens.

The Greek city, located in an area called Attica, was ruled by King Cecrops (SEE-krops). He was either born of a dragon[1] or perhaps just sprang from the earth. While his top half was human, including his face and arms, his bottom half resembled a serpent's tail. Cecrops had introduced the customs of burial, marriage, reading, and writing to the citizens of Attica. Now he was about to do something else for his people.

Both Athena (uh-THEE-nuh), the goddess of war and wisdom, and Poseidon (poh-SY-dun), the god of the sea, had watched the area's development. Each wanted to be the deity that the city worshiped—but only one god would get the job. Which one would be chosen?

Someone—perhaps Cecrops—suggested they hold a contest. Whichever god offered the best gift would be the patron deity of the city. Cecrops would be the judge.

With a large flock of citizens following, the two gods and the king went to the Acropolis. Poseidon stepped forward and struck the rock of the Acropolis with his trident. Instantly the rock split open, and water gushed forth. (Another story says that a horse appeared when Poseidon struck the earth with his trident,[2] but the more common version is that of the water.) Cecrops tasted the water as Poseidon stood smugly by, confident that he had won the contest for the people's affection. But Cecrops judged the water to be salty. It was unsuitable for drinking, cooking, or even bathing.

Then it was Athena's turn. She stepped forward and struck the ground with her spear. From that place sprouted an olive tree. The olives could be eaten, the oil used for cooking, and the wood used for fire. Athena had devised a very useful gift indeed.

Cecrops declared Athena the winner of the contest. The city—which would be known as Athens in her honor—was hers. Naturally, Poseidon was not pleased with this outcome. He sent raging waters to flood Attica.

According to mythology expert Edith Hamilton, in another version of this story, a casualty of the contest between the two gods was the rights of women.[3] In those early days, the women of Attica had the right to vote, just like the men. All the women voted for Athena's gift, while all the men voted for Poseidon's. Since the women numbered one more than the men, Athena won the vote. Outraged, the

The Contest between Athena and Poseidon, created by Antonio Fantuzzi around 1543. The artist depicts Athena with her gift of the olive tree, and Poseidon with his gift of the horse. Other versions of the myth say his gift was a saltwater spring.

men of Attica decided to take away the women's right to vote. This is why women could not vote in ancient Greece.

Yet another version finds this dispute between god and goddess settled on Mount Olympus in a type of court in which Cecrops was called to give evidence. Zeus (ZOOS), the king of the gods, took no part in the final decision, but the goddesses voted for Athena and all the other gods for Poseidon. Athena won in this version also.[4]

No matter which version is told, the story shows Poseidon as a god who did not take defeat lightly. One of the most powerful of all the Olympians, he ruled the universe with Zeus, who was his brother. Although he was important in the Greek pantheon (the entire group of gods and goddesses), Poseidon almost wasn't born.

The tale of Poseidon's birth started long ago, with the union of Gaia (GY-uh), Mother Earth, and Uranus (YOO-ruh-nus), the Sky. The two of them fell in love and had children. The first of these were monsters—beings with one hundred hands and fifty heads. Three others were called the Cyclopes (sy-KLOH-peez) because each had only one glowing eye in the middle of his forehead. (In later myths, at least one Cyclops is the son of Poseidon.) All of these children were as big as mountains and powerfully strong. Uranus was not pleased with their appearance. Then Gaia gave birth to the Titans. They were also huge and strong, but they were not monsters or destructive like the others. Some, in fact, would turn out to be helpful.

Uranus hated the hundred-handers—so much so that he seized them and imprisoned them in Tartarus, a dark and desolate place deep inside Mother Earth. This pained and saddened Gaia, for she loved all her children. She made a sickle out of the hardest flint, then begged her sons the Titans to use the sickle to attack Uranus and set their brothers in Tartarus free.

The Titans trembled at this request, for Uranus was supremely powerful. Only the youngest and strongest Titan, Cronus, was bold enough to take the sickle. He attacked Uranus and severely wounded him. From Uranus' blood sprang another race, the Giants.

Cronus was now the lord of the universe—though as a father he was not much better than Uranus. He did not keep his word to Gaia to free his brothers from Tartarus. After marrying Rhea (REE-uh), Cronus learned that one of his sons would someday overthrow him, just as he had overthrown his father. To avoid his fate, each time Rhea gave birth to a child, Cronus swallowed it. He figured that with the children safely inside him, he had nothing to fear. One of those he swallowed was Poseidon.

Rhea, with the help of Gaia, tricked Cronus. The next time Rhea gave birth, she hid the baby—whose name was Zeus—and gave Cronus a stone wrapped in a blanket to swallow. He did so, and thought he was safe. Rhea took baby Zeus and hid him in a secret cave on the island of Crete. Gaia helped keep him hidden from Cronus by setting up noisy spirits outside the cave. Their constant commotion disguised the baby's crying.

Eventually Zeus grew to manhood and challenged Cronus. But before he could confront his father, Zeus' wife, Metis, gave Cronus a magic herb, telling him it would make him invincible. Instead it made him sick. He vomited up all the children he had swallowed, among them Poseidon, who joined Zeus and the other gods to defeat Cronus.

Poseidon became a valuable and powerful ally of Zeus in the wars that followed. Finally, when all the wars were over and the Olympians were in control of the universe, the three brothers—Zeus, Poseidon, and Hades (HAY-deez)—drew lots to see what part of the world they would rule. Zeus became the supreme god and master of the sky. Hades became lord of the Underworld, and went there to live. Poseidon became king of the waters. Instead of always living on Mount Olympus—part of the earthly domain the three would share—he kept an underwater palace off the eastern coast of Greece. He is usually depicted in myths as quick to anger. This is why, in a fit of rage, he sent a flood to Attica after he lost its newest city to Athena.

Athena

Athena was one of the twelve main Greek gods. She changed the orientation of the myths from one gender to the other.

According to legend, Zeus was told he would have a son who would be mightier than he and replace him. To avoid this fate, he swallowed his first wife, Metis (MEE-tis), so that she could not give birth. One day, while walking along the shore of a lake, Zeus was struck with the most intense headache he had ever felt. Indeed, the pain was so bad that he roared in agony, which brought the other gods rushing to his aid. Unable to endure the pain, Zeus asked Hephaestus (heh-FES-tus), the god of

The Birth of Athena

fire, to split his skull open with an ax. Reluctantly, Hephaestus did so. When his ax struck Zeus' head, Athena stepped out of it, dressed in full body armor, with a shout that was heard around the world.

With the story of Athena's birth, the theme of the Greek stories switched from one dominated by women to one dominated by men. Athena had no mother; she was born directly from the head of Zeus. By the same token, Zeus did not need a woman to give birth to Athena. The earliest creation myths, as told in chapter one, prominently featured females who defeated males. With the birth of Athena, that balance shifted.

Athena became one of Zeus' favorites. She was the goddess of war, wisdom, and the arts. Although she wore armor, she was not vicious and bloodthirsty like her half brother Ares, the god of war. Athena usually preferred to find peaceful resolutions to conflicts. Yet when necessary, she could be a fierce fighter.

A unique combination of intelligence and strength, Athena often rewarded those qualities in mortals. She helped Perseus kill the Gorgon Medusa when all who had tried before him had been turned to stone. (Athena later put Medusa's head in the center of her shield.) She also helped Odysseus during his long quest to return home from the battlefields of Troy. The Romans worshiped Athena as Minerva.

A fourth-century Roman mosaic shows Neptune driving a sea chariot. He was associated with horses and with hippocamps—creatures that were half horse and half sea serpent. They pulled his chariot over the waters.

POSEIDON

CHAPTER 2

Poseidon's Family Tree

The ancient Greeks were a seafaring people, so Poseidon, the god of the sea, held an important place in their mythology. He could command the ocean to be stormy or calm, and when he rode over the waters in his great golden chariot, all storminess ceased and peaceful conditions followed in his wake. Poseidon was married to Amphitrite (am-fih-TRY-tee), a granddaughter of Ocean, one of the Titans. Often Poseidon was depicted as looking haggard and weary, as if he were carrying all the world's worries.

Besides his role as god of the sea—which also included freshwater rivers and lakes—Poseidon was recognized for giving the first horse to mankind. Because of this gift, the Greeks honored him before horse races. Bulls were also sacred to the sea god. During certain festivals that were dedicated to Poseidon, black bulls were thrown into the waves.[1]

Sometimes called "earth-shaker,"[2] Poseidon was usually pictured carrying a spear with three prongs called a trident. His trident was an all-purpose weapon: He could throw it, shatter things with it, or slam it into the ground to cause earthquakes.

Despite his position in the Greek pantheon, Poseidon may have been worshiped even earlier than Zeus was. According to researcher Félix Guirand, "His province, later confined to the waters, was in primitive times much wider."[3] He also defines part of Poseidon's name as "to be master,"[4] indicating that at some point he was the supreme deity in charge of everything—a sort of "pre-Zeus."

Guirand speculates that the trident Poseidon always carried was at one time perhaps a thunderbolt, or a symbol of a thunderbolt.[5]

A statue of Poseidon with his trident watches over a port in Copenhagen, Denmark.

Indeed, there is a very strong physical resemblance between Poseidon and Zeus in the way the ancient Greeks portrayed them in their art. A famous statue of Poseidon now in a museum in Athens was once believed to be that of Zeus.[6]

"Poseidon was a national god of the Ionians of the Peloponnese [a large peninsula in southern Greece], who brought him with them when they emigrated from Asia,"[7] wrote Guirand. He said that worship of Poseidon was quite extensive in this part of Greece, even to the point that the god was called *Genethlios*, or "Creator," in Sparta,[8] which is located on the Peloponnesian peninsula.

Poseidon's three-pronged trident was particularly appropriate for him to carry. It resembled the multi-pronged spear that Mediterranean fishermen used as late as the 1960s.[9] Poseidon's trident gradually became a symbol of domination of the seas, and countries and rulers who liked to boast of their mastery of the water used it as a symbol. Great Britain, for example, once the mightiest sea-power on earth, placed an image of Britannia, the personification of their country, holding Poseidon's trident on the back of its penny.[10]

One characteristic of Poseidon was that he always seemed to envy the earthly possessions of his fellow gods—such as

British penny

There were many similarities between Zeus and Poseidon, not the least of which was their appearance. This statue of Poseidon, in Athens, was once thought to be that of Zeus. His hand probably once held a trident.

Athena's dominion in Athens. He also quarreled with Hera (HAYR-uh) over who would get Argolis, an area near the Aegean Sea. Poseidon lost this match too, and took his revenge by drying up the area's three main rivers. He unsuccessfully fought with Zeus over an island called Aegina, and with Dionysus for another island named Naxos.

Initially Poseidon had been interested in making Thetis (THEE-tiss) his wife. She was a Nereid—a sea nymph or mermaid. Then he heard a prediction that any son born to Thetis would be greater than his father.[11] Poseidon was well aware of what could happen when a son became mightier than his father—as Zeus had shown with Cronus—so he did not pursue her. (She married a mortal named Peleus [PEE-lee-us]; their son would be the Greek hero Achilles.)

Next Poseidon turned his attention to Amphitrite, another Nereid. As he watched her dancing with her sisters on the island of Naxos, he fell in love with her. When Poseidon first asked her to marry him, she refused and ran away. Poseidon sent Delphinus to find her and bring her back to him. When he did so, Poseidon rewarded him by placing his image among the stars as the Dolphin constellation.

Thus did Poseidon and Amphitrite join together as husband and wife. From then on Amphitrite shared Poseidon's watery kingdom.

The Triumph of Neptune and Amphitrite by Frans Francken II. It took Poseidon a long time to convince Amphitrite to marry him. Once he did, however, she stayed by his side as his loyal and faithful wife.

Sometimes they rode along the waves together on his golden chariot, with Amphitrite blowing on conch shells. Sometimes she held Poseidon's trident as he maneuvered his fabulous team of horses.

Unfortunately for Amphitrite, Poseidon, like his brother Zeus, was not a faithful companion. Even after he was married, he continued to have affairs with other women. However, although Poseidon was much like Zeus, Amphitrite was nothing like Zeus' wife, Hera. The many affairs of Zeus made the jealous Hera furious, and Greek mythology is filled with tales of how she took revenge on some poor woman who had been with her husband. Most of the time, Amphitrite, however, was the opposite of Hera. She patiently put up with Poseidon's many infidelities. But one time Amphitrite did show jealousy, and she exacted terrible vengeance. Poseidon had been with Scylla (SIH-luh), a nymph of extraordinary beauty. Amphitrite became

Scylla the Six-Headed Monster, by Henry Justice Ford, published in 1907. In Ford's depiction, Scylla's heads have tentacles with which to grab her victims.

extremely jealous of the kind and loving manner in which Poseidon treated her, so she plotted revenge. There was a pool in which Scylla would bathe, and into this pool Amphitrite threw magic herbs. The next time Scylla stepped into the pool, she turned into a horrible monster with six heads and twelve feet.

There is another version of that story that does not include either Poseidon or Amphitrite. According to that version, the beautiful Scylla denied the advances of a half-man, half-fish named Glaucus (GLAW-kus). In despair, Glaucus went to Circe

(SIR-see, or KIR-kee), the enchantress, to get a love potion to use on Scylla. But as he told Circe his story, she fell in love with him. No matter what Circe said or did, Glaucus could not be persuaded to love her back. Furious, the enchantress prepared a powerful potion that she threw into the water. The moment Scylla stepped into the pool, she turned into a horrible monster.[12] It seems that poor Scylla was doomed to become a monster no matter what!

Scylla and Glaucus, painted by Bartholomeus Spranger in 1581. In both versions of the Scylla story—the one featuring Poseidon and the one featuring Glaucus—Scylla was a nymph whose beauty drew vengeful jealousy.

Triton Blowing on a Conch Shell, created by Jacques de Gheyn III around 1615. Triton was the son of Poseidon and Amphitrite.

From the union of Poseidon and Amphitrite there came two daughters and one son. The daughters were Rhode (the island of Rhodes was named after her) and Benthesicyme (ben-thih-sih-KY-mee). The son was Triton—a merman with green hair, scales, the upper body of a human, and the lower body of a fish.

Neptune

The ancient Romans adopted many of the Greek gods into their own mythology. While their names were usually different, they had similar characteristics to their Greek counterparts. The Roman god who was similar to the Greek god Poseidon was Neptune; his wife was Salacia (equivalent to Amphitrite). Overall, Neptune was not as important a god as Poseidon, nor did he play as prominent a role in the life of Rome's people.

In the beginning, Neptune was usually identified with a female who, it is believed, was the goddess of salt water. At first, ancient Romans would thank the god Fortunus for naval victories and other sea-going successes, but by the first century BCE, Neptune had become the primary Roman sea god. For example, around that time a Roman general referred to himself as Neptune's son.

Neptune calms the stormy seas, from Virgil's *Aeneid,* the story of the Trojan hero Aeneas and the founding of Rome. Juno (the Roman name for Hera) calls the winds to toss about the ships of Aeneas and his men. Neptune, furious that the winds have raised the storm without consulting him, banishes the winds, and fair weather returns. Aeneas can then continue his quest.

The Romans built two temples for Neptune. The first was near a racetrack. This made sense, because, like Poseidon, Neptune was considered the god of horses, and was sometimes called Neptune Equester. The second temple was built to celebrate a great Roman naval victory at Actium.

Romans held a major festival in Neptune's honor in the heat and drought of late July called the Neptunalia. At this time committees of citizens could vote on criminal or civil legal matters. Not much is known about this festival except that the Romans would build huts constructed of branches and foliage for the holiday. It is also possible that athletic games were played at this time.

Ancient Greece was composed of many city-states, of which Athens was one of the most important and most powerful. Each city-state had its own independent government. With its numerous islands and miles of shoreline, ancient Greece relied on the sea—and on the kindness of Poseidon.

POSEIDON

CHAPTER 3

Everyday Greek Life

Just as people are today, the ancient Greeks were curious about the natural world. They asked such questions as, Why do mountains seem to echo? Why and how does the sun move across the sky? Why do the seasons change? How was the world created? These types of questions were all addressed by myths. The tales were an effort to explain the world in terms the Greeks could understand. Myths also attempted to explain more personal aspects of life, such as what love is or what happens to those who commit a crime. For these reasons, Greek myths are more than just entertaining tales of gods and goddesses—they are teaching tools that helped the average Greek person make sense of ordinary life. Shipwrecks and extreme weather such as hurricanes and flooding were blamed on the gods. Sometimes Poseidon caused these catastrophes when he was angry; sometimes he caused them when another god needed his help in punishing mortals.

The story of the Lesser Ajax (who was not the same person as the Great Ajax, a hero in the Trojan War, but who fought alongside him) is one example of how the Greeks explained shipwrecks and deadly storms. At the end of the Trojan War, when the Greeks were sacking Troy, the prophetess Cassandra took refuge at a statue of Athena. Ajax (also spelled Aias) found her there and attacked her. The Greeks voted to stone him for his crime, but he escaped death by praying at Athena's altar. Athena was outraged by his behavior—and by the other Greek sailors who did not punish him for it. She asked Zeus and Poseidon to help her sink their ships.

Like many of the myths, the story of Ajax is recounted by Homer. In Homer's *Odyssey*, the Old Man of the sea tells the hero

Odysseus what happened when Poseidon stepped in to help Athena ruin Ajax and his companions:

> First of all Poseidon drove him against the great rocks
> of Gyrai, and yet he saved him out of the water,
> and Aias would have escaped his doom, though [Athena]
>   hated him,
> had he not gone wildly mad and tossed out a word of defiance;
> for he said that in despite of the gods he escaped the great gulf
> of the sea, and Poseidon heard him, loudly vaunting [boasting],
> and at once with his ponderous hands catching up the trident
> he drove it against the Gyrean rock, and split a piece of it,
> and part of it stayed where it was, but a splinter crashed
>   in the water,
> and this was where Aias had been perched when he raved
>   so madly.
> It carried him down to the depths of the endless and tossing
>   main sea.
> So Aias died, when he had swallowed down the salt water.[1]

From Homer, we learn much about the lives of soldiers and sailors, and the gods' hand in them, but what was ordinary life like? How did the ancient Greeks live? Were they like present-day people, or were there great differences?

Let's start with the typical Greek house. The Greeks were capable of constructing magnificent public buildings, such as the Parthenon in Athens, a temple built for Athena. However, it seems that they did not give their private homes as much effort. Typically, a private home had a stone foundation and walls made of sun-baked bricks. These walls were not very strong, however; burglars were known as "wall-piercers" because they could apparently bore right through the bricks.[2] Many houses had outside courtyards, in which household chores such as cooking were done. The rooms were not

Ajax and Cassandra, painted by Solomon Joseph Solomon in 1886. When Ajax angered Athena by attacking Cassandra, Poseidon helped Athena get revenge.

very big, and usually had earthen floors. Some houses built by the wealthy had stone floors. The furnishings were sparse by our standards, consisting of a chest, couch, chairs and stools, and tables.

Clothing was simple and quickly put on. Men wore a linen shirt called a chiton, possibly topped by a woolen cloak called a himation, and sandals.[3] Women wore a longer, dresslike version of the chiton that was fastened by shoulder brooches or a belt. Women also wore himations.

The main meal was usually in late afternoon. Other eating times were in the morning and at midday, but these were more like snacks than meals. Bread and fish were commonly on the menu; vegetables, eggs, olives, grapes, and figs were also sometimes served. Milk and cheese came from goats, and honey was used as a sweetener. People usually ate with knives and their fingers. A family may have prayed to Poseidon before eating if they had a family member on a ship at sea.

Men were the dominant force in Greek life. Women could not vote and played almost no role in politics, while social events were usually reserved for men also. Women were not even allowed into the main area of the Olympic games. Females participated in their own games, which were minor compared to the Olympics.

Women primarily stayed home, did the household chores, and raisied the children. When babies were born, the healthy and strong

The Olympic Games, which began in ancient Greece, honored Zeus. The Greeks also held a similar event called the Isthmian Games. These games honored Poseidon and featured chariot races, and women may have been allowed to participate.

ones were welcomed with open arms. The sick and weak ones were often put in a clay pot and left outside someplace to die of exposure to the elements.[4] This practice was a common feature in the Greek myths. Even the children of gods could be left to die. For example, Poseidon's son Hippothoon was abandoned as an infant.

While boys went to school, girls did not; they were taught how to perform household tasks by their mother, and they often got married around age fifteen. A daughter's parents usually arranged her marriage, and it was not uncommon for a bride to get her first look at her new husband on the day of her wedding.

Women had a multitude of things to do in running the household. Besides taking care of the children, a woman had to buy corn, take it home, grind it, and bake it into bread. Water had to be carried home from the public fountain, no matter how far. There were

The Temple of Poseidon at Cape Sounion near Athens, Greece, is believed to have once had on its walls figures depicting the sea god's battle with Athena over control of Athens. Standing high on a bluff over the Aegean Sea, the temple would have been the ideal place to make sacrifices to Poseidon when asking for safe passage over the sea. It would have also given sailors comfort to have Poseidon watching over them as they left for war or returned to harbor.

clothes to make or repair, cleaning, buying items at market, and cooking.

Many households had slaves to help with the chores. By one estimate, there were between 80,000 and 100,000 slaves in Athens in the fifth century BCE, or nearly one slave to every three free people.[5] A household could have one or two slaves, or in the case of General Nikias, a thousand. (He used them as a business, hiring them out to work in the mines.)

If all this work made a person hot, tired, and dirty, they could always go to a public bath to refresh themselves. The public baths were ideal places to talk and gossip with friends while washing. It's likely that the water came up only to a person's hip, but it was certainly preferable to trying to wash at home from water in basins.

The Greeks were a seafaring people, which is why Poseidon was such an important god to them. Greece is surrounded by water, making the sea a major part of its culture. The Greeks were constantly on the lookout for new trading opportunities with other countries along the Mediterranean coast, and they also sought to settle new cities there. By the seventh and sixth centuries BCE, the Greeks had established a string of settlements stretching from western Asia Minor all the way to the coasts of modern-day Spain and France.

In no Greek city-state was the water more important than in Athens. The city increased its seagoing power through both a brisk commercial trade and naval leadership until it had become the mightiest Greek presence on the water. Athenian trade ships used for commercial purposes were rounded, single-masted craft with a deep hold.[6] They were small (an average length of 20 meters, or about 65 feet) and slow (with the wind behind them they traveled at a top speed of five knots, which is about 5.7 miles per hour.)[7] Worst of all, they were unsafe. Captains had no charts, compasses, lighthouses, or buoys to help them navigate, so they sailed only during daylight hours and hugged the coastline. This made the ships prone to hitting sandbars and other underwater obstructions that typically lurk just offshore.

Since these types of ships were so unsafe, yet so important to the economy of Athens and all of Greece, it's little wonder that sailors on board prayed to Poseidon for a safe journey and calm seas. Yet it's also remarkable that, as busy as he was with all of his romantic encounters, Poseidon heard these prayers at all.

Athenian trade ship

Isthmian Games

Silver jug, Isthmian Games,
first century CE

The Isthmus of Corinth, which connects the Peloponnesian peninsula with the mainland of Greece, is located between the Gulf of Corinth and the Saronic Gulf. It was on this stretch of land that the ancient Greeks held the Isthmian Games, with Poseidon playing a key role in the festivities.

As well as being sandwiched by the sea, the Isthmus of Corinth is affected by frequent earthquakes, so it was natural that Poseidon, with the earthshaking ability of his mighty trident, was the god of the isthmus. In addition, he was associated with horses, and much of the Isthmian Games centered around horse racing. The games were held in the year before and the year after the Olympic Games.

There are several myths that explain how the Isthmian Games began. The Corinthians claimed that the games began to honor the boy Melicertes, who died when his mother Ino ran away from her husband, King Athamas of Orchomenus. To escape Athamas, Ino jumped into the Saronic Gulf with the boy in her arms. She was turned into a sea goddess named Leucothea, and he was transformed into the sea deity Palaemon. A dolphin carried Melicertes' body back to the isthmus. At his funeral, Sisyphus, the king of Corinth, held the first Isthmian Games in his honor.

However, the Athenians credited the founding of the games to the legendary Theseus. According to the story, Theseus came upon the murderer Sinis on the isthmus, who challenged him to a pine-bending contest. Theseus defeated Sinis, and celebrated his victory by establishing the Isthmian Games.

Athletes from all over Greece attended these games. Before they began, everyone involved in the contests had to swear on the Altar of Poseidon that they would play by the rules and use no unlawful means to win. Besides horse racing, the games may have included boat races that could not begin before dedications were made to Poseidon. Musical contests and torch racing may also have been part of the games. Winners received a wreath of pine. Later, wreaths made of wild celery were also awarded.

The Perseus Series: The Death of Medusa I, created by Sir Edward Coley Burnes-Jones in 1882. When Perseus killed Medusa, two offspring of Poseidon, the fabulous Pegasus and Chrysaor, were born from her blood.

POSEIDON

CHAPTER 4

The Many Loves of Poseidon

Like Zeus, Poseidon was known for fathering many children with females who were not his wife. Some of these children could walk on water, and some became heroes who fought at Troy or joined Jason on the *Argo*. One of his sons was Theseus, the great Greek hero who killed the Minotaur. Being the object of Poseidon's love could bring a woman mountains of trouble, but whereas Hera took revenge on her husband's lovers, Amphitrite didn't have to do much of anything to them. Bad luck seemed to follow these women around even without her intervention. One of the victims was Medusa (muh-DOO-suh).

Medusa had once been a beautiful maiden. She turned away all the men who wanted to be with her, but finally she agreed to be with Poseidon. Some say that Poseidon came to her in the shape of a horse or bird and seduced her in that way.[1] Medusa compounded her mistake by being with Poseidon in a temple dedicated to Athena. This enraged the goddess, who quite possibly had been jealous of Medusa's great beauty anyway.[2] Athena thus transformed Medusa into a hideous, ugly monster.

Medusa became a Gorgon, one of three scowling sisters with glaring eyes; tongues like a snake's flicking out between long, sharp teeth; claws hard as metal; and serpents for hair. A Gorgon could turn a person into stone just by looking at them. The Gorgons' faces were so fierce that Greek bakers used to paint their images on their oven doors. They hoped to scare people from opening the door and peeking inside, thereby cooling the ovens and ruining the baking bread.[3] The Gorgons' names were Stheno ("Strong"), Euryale ("Wide-roaming"), and Medusa ("Cunning One"). Of the three, only Medusa could be killed; her two sisters were immortal.

Medusa and her sisters fled to a place at the end of the earth, where neither the sun nor moon ever shone. There they lived in a cave, which became littered with the stone statues of men who tried to kill Medusa and failed. Finally the great hero Perseus (PER-see-us) came to this place to kill Medusa by cutting off her head. He succeeded because two gods aided him. Athena guided his hand, and Hermes gave him his winged sandals and other gifts.

What Perseus did not know was that Medusa was pregnant from the night she'd spent with Poseidon. From the blood that escaped when Perseus cut off her head arose two creatures: Pegasus (PEH-guh-sus), the winged horse; and Chrysaor (krih-SAY-or), who became a warrior.

After slaying Medusa, Perseus was not yet clear of Poseidon. As he flew home with his winged sandals over the coast of Ethiopia, with the head of Medusa in a bag, he saw a beautiful woman chained to a rock below. He landed next to her and heard her story.

Her name was Andromeda (an-DRAH-muh-duh), and she was the daughter of Queen Cassiopeia (kaa-see-oh-PEE-uh) of Ethiopia. The queen had foolishly boasted that she was more beautiful than the Nereids, who attended Poseidon. As Edith Hamilton pointed out: "An absolutely certain way in those days to draw down on one a wretched fate was to claim superiority in anything over any deity."[4] Sure enough, Poseidon had taken offense at Cassiopeia's remark. He flooded Ethiopia and sent a sea monster to wreak havoc there. Ethiopia's King Cepheus had learned from an oracle that the only way he could satisfy Poseidon and save his kingdom was to offer his daughter Andromeda as a sacrifice to the sea monster. He chained the girl to a rock by the water.

As he listened to her story, Perseus fell in love with Andromeda. He decided to fight the sea monster. When it emerged from the water seeking its prey, Perseus jumped onto its head. The battle

Perseus and Andromeda, painted by Pierre Mignard in 1679. In anger, Poseidon sent a sea monster to ravage the countryside, then demanded that Andromeda be its victim. Perseus arrived to rescue her.

between the two took some time, but when it was over, the monster was dead. Perseus and Andromeda lived happily ever after.

Poseidon contributed to another important myth when he became involved with the goddess Demeter (DIH-mih-ter).

Demeter was the goddess of the harvest, and of all living, growing things. She had a daughter named Persephone (pur-SEF-uh-nee), and the two were very close. When Demeter came down from Olympus to check on the plants of the earth, lovely Persephone went with her. Wherever Persephone danced, flowers sprang from the ground.

Hades, lord of the Underworld, also noticed Persephone. He fell in love with her and wanted to make her his queen. But since he knew that Demeter would never agree to let her daughter be with him, Hades decided to kidnap the child. One day on earth, when Persephone had wandered away from her mother, Hades rose up through a crack in the ground, grabbed her, and took her back to the Underworld with him. When Demeter went to look for her daughter, she couldn't find her anywhere. The more she searched, the more tired and depressed she became.

At this point Poseidon appeared. He wanted to be with Demeter, but Demeter was so discouraged that she rejected any romantic relationship at the time. Poseidon persisted, so Demeter turned herself into a mare, hoping to trick him. She went to graze with a herd of horses owned by one of Apollo's sons. Poseidon was not fooled. He transformed himself into a stallion and made love to Demeter. The goddess was so mad that in that region she was known forevermore as Demeter the Fury.[5]

From the union of Poseidon and Demeter came two children: a nymph whose name may have been Despoina, and a wild horse named Areion. (The real name of Despoina, which means "Mistress," was unknown except to those few who participated in secret rituals for her.) Areion's right feet were human, and he could talk.

(The end of the story of Demeter and Persephone is that Demeter became so grief-stricken that she neglected the growing things on the earth, and all the plants died. Zeus finally had to intervene and ruled that

The Return of Persephone by Frederic Leighton, 1891. Leighton depicts Hermes helping Persephone to return to her mother, Demeter.

Demeter could have her daughter back, but only if Persephone had not eaten any food in Hades. Unfortunately Persephone had, so a compromise was reached: Persephone could spend half the year with Demeter and half with Hades. When the girl is with Demeter, the earth is warm and green; and when she is with Hades, the world is barren and cold. The story explains the changing of the seasons.)

Another woman with whom Poseidon had an affair was Theophane (thee-AH-fah-nee). She was a great beauty, and many men wanted to be with her. In order to keep her all for himself, Poseidon carried her to the island of Crinissa. Unfortunately for him, Theophane's many suitors followed her there. Poseidon turned Theophane and the rest of the island's inhabitants into sheep. Thus disguised, it was impossible for the suitors to find the girl. Poseidon then changed himself into a ram and lay down with Theophane. She became pregnant, and gave birth to a ram that had a fleece of gold. It was this ram's fleece that Jason and the Argonauts journeyed to find.

Poseidon also seduced a woman named Chione (KY-oh-nee). She became pregnant and had a son named Eumolpus (yoo-MUL-pus). Ashamed by the child, Chione threw him into the sea. Poseidon rescued the baby

Poseidon approached Theophane disguised as a ram. Their offspring would grow a golden fleece.

and took him to his daughter Benthesicyme, who raised the boy. Eumolpus would later co-found the Eleusinian Mysteries, a festival honoring Demeter that included fasting, performing dramatic plays, and purifying rituals.

A far worse fate awaited a woman called Alope (AL-oh-pee), who also had an affair with Poseidon and consequently had a son by him. Alope covered the baby with a robe and left him outside to die. Fortunately a mare came by—probably sent by Poseidon—and fed the infant. Some shepherds found the baby and brought him to Cercyon (SER-see-on), Alope's father and king of Eleusis. Cercyon recognized the robe as one of his family's, and in that way discovered that the baby was his daughter's. He imprisoned her forever, and again put the baby outside to die. Once again, the mare came to feed him and saved his life. The baby grew to be called Hippothoon ("Horse Swift"). Years later, when Theseus killed Cercyon, Hippothoon became king of Eleusis in his place.

Poseidon also loved the nymph Tyro, but she rejected his advances. He didn't think that he would ever be able to be with her. Tyro became quite fond of the river Enipeus and spent a lot of time by it. This gave Poseidon an idea. One day, when she was walking along the riverbanks, Poseidon appeared to her as the god of the river. He suggested that they become lovers. Tyro, fooled by Poseidon's disguise, agreed. This relationship produced two sons, Pelias and Neleus.[6] Tyro abandoned her children, but they were found and raised by a horse breeder. They later rescued their mother from her evil stepmother.[7] She married Cretheus, king of Iolcus, and gave birth to Aeson and two other sons. Pelias and Aeson's son Jason would vie for the throne of Iolcus, setting the stage for Jason's quest for the golden fleece.

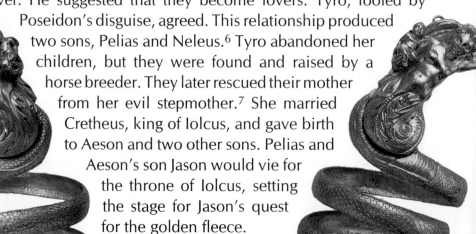

Triton armbands
c.200 BCE

Jason and the Argonauts

The story of Jason's quest for the golden fleece is one of the most thrilling in Greek mythology. When he reached adulthood, Jason returned to the kingdom of Iolcus in northern Greece to restore the throne to his father, Aeson. Years earlier, Pelias had usurped the throne from Aeson, who was Pelias' half brother. Pelias said he would give up the throne if Jason would find and retrieve the fabulous golden fleece.

Jason brings Pelias the Golden Fleece

Jason agreed and assembled the finest crew in all of Greece for his ship, the *Argo*. Among its members were the legendary hero Hercules; Poseidon's son Euphemus, who could walk on water; Periclymenus, another of Poseidon's sons who could change his form during battle; and Orpheus, a son of the god Apollo. They called themselves the Argonauts after their ship.

On their voyage to obtain the fleece, the crew encountered an island populated only by women, and they were nearly seduced by them into remaining there permanently. They fought a group of six-armed giants, battled people they mistook for pirates, and subdued the Harpies—horrible bird women—so that a starving king could eat again. They also managed to slip the ship through a group of boulders that crashed together to crush anything between them. Jason single-handedly killed an entire group of men that sprouted from dragon's teeth thrown on the ground. Finding the fleece guarded by a dragon, Jason made the creature fall asleep, then snatched his prize.

The journey home was filled with more adventures, including storms, schemes, and trickery by some of the gods. Eventually Jason and almost all of the Argonauts survived to bring the golden fleece back home. Pelias went back on his word and refused to give up the throne (he had poisoned Aeson), so Jason's new wife, the sorceress Medea, persuaded Pelias' own daughters to kill him. Pelias' son Acastus took the throne.

Odysseus pours wine for Polyphemus the Cyclops. Odysseus was cunning enough to save most of his men from Polyphemus, but his actions also angered Poseidon. The Greeks' unfortunate landing on the Island of the Cyclopes, the sons of Poseidon, would doom their return from Troy.

POSEIDON

CHAPTER 5

Tales of Poseidon

In some Greek myths, Poseidon plays a part but is not the main character. One of these is the *Odyssey*—the epic story of Odysseus' long journey home.

Odysseus, one of the mightiest of the Greek warriors, was away from home fighting the Trojan War for ten years. At last, with the war over and Greece victorious, he and his men started their voyage home to Ithaca. It would take ten more adventure-filled years to get there.

In one of their adventures, Odysseus and his men encountered a mountainous island with unnaturally bountiful crops. Wheat, barley, vines fat with grapes—these plants and others grew lushly all about. However, no people could be seen.

There was a great cave high up in one of the mountains. Leaving the rest of his crew behind, Odysseus took twelve men and went to explore it. He also took a wineskin with him. The cave was filled with sheep and great baskets of food, such as cheese. Shortly, the owner of the cave returned. It was Poseidon's son Polyphemus (pah-lih-FEE-mus), a Cyclops—a giant with only a single eye in the middle of his forehead. He rolled a great boulder across the opening in the front of the cave. Odysseus asked for his hospitality in the name of Zeus. In response, the Cyclops crushed and ate two of Odysseus' men, then went to sleep. Odysseus was tempted to kill him as he slept, but he reconsidered when he looked at the boulder blocking the doorway. The Greeks could never move it themselves. They were trapped.

In the morning, Polyphemus ate two more of Odysseus' men, then went out to tend his sheep, being careful to put the boulder back in place as he left. While he was gone, the Greeks sharpened a log to a point, like a pencil. That night the Cyclops killed and ate two more of the Greeks. When the monster was finished, Odysseus stepped forth and held up his wineskin.

"Here, Cyclops, have a drink of wine," he said, "now you have fed on human flesh."[1]

The wine was very strong and very good, and the giant was pleased. Polyphemus asked Odysseus his name.

"Noman is my name,"[2] Odysseus replied. The Cyclops said that as a reward for the wine, he would eat Odysseus last. Then he fell into a drunken sleep. As he slept, Odysseus and his remaining men drove the sharpened log into the giant's eye, blinding him. The creature jumped up with a roar that was heard by his brother Cyclopes in nearby caves. When they called to Polyphemus and asked what was happening, he replied, "Noman is killing me!"[3] When the other Cyclopes heard that, they thought their brother was just having a bad dream and went back to sleep.

In the morning the blinded Cyclops rolled away the boulder to let his sheep out. He felt the top of each animal to make sure that the Greeks weren't riding them. Little did he suspect that they were clinging to the bellies of the sheep.

Once the Greeks escaped and got back on their ship—sheep and all—they began quickly rowing away. Odysseus couldn't resist taunting Polyphemus. From his ship he hollered, "Cyclops, if any mortal man should ask you [who took your sight], tell him that you were blinded by Odysseus, sacker of cities!"[4]

When the Cyclops heard that, he shouted, "Hear you that, my father. Prove me your son, oh, great earth-shaking Poseidon, and avenge me. . . . Bear him away from his home, and in your murky depths bury his foul companions."[5]

Poseidon heard his son's prayer, and from that moment on he plagued Odysseus' journey with ill winds, storms, and rough seas. Indeed, at one point the Greeks were so close to Ithaca they could

Ulysses in the Cave of Polyphemus, painted by Jacob Jordaens in the 1630s. The Romans knew the Greek hero Odysseus as Ulysses. Jordaens shows the men escaping by crawling along the floor under Polyphemus' sheep.

see figures on the beach, but Poseidon kept knocking them off course. It took many more years and adventures before Odysseus was able to return home. His companions never made it.

Ironically, Poseidon had been on the side of the Greeks during the Trojan War. Long before, in disguise, Poseidon had helped build the walls for the city of Troy for King Laomedon (lay-OH-mih-don). The king had promised Poseidon a reward for his work, but when the walls were done, Laomedon went back on his word and refused to pay. He didn't realize he was cheating a god in disguise.

Another tale in which Poseidon played a prominent role was that of Erysichthon (ayr-ih-SIK-thon).

Erysichthon made the foolish mistake of cutting down a tree in a grove sacred to Demeter. So angry was the goddess that she sent

Famine to take possession of Erysichthon, so that no matter how much he ate, he would always be hungry. From that day forth, Erysichthon ate continually. He spent all his money on vast amounts of food, but still felt hungry. He sold everything he owned to buy more food, but that didn't satisfy him. Finally he had nothing left to sell but his daughter Mestra, so he sold her too—into slavery.

As she waited on the beach to be transported to her owner's ship, Mestra prayed to Poseidon to save her from a life of slavery. The god heard her prayer and changed her into a fisherman. When her owner saw only the figure of a fisherman on the beach, he asked where the girl who was there a moment ago had gone. The "fisherman" answered, "I swear by the God of the Sea that no man except myself has come to this shore, and no woman either."[6] The slaveowner went back to his boat, still baffled, and left. As soon as he was gone, Mestra returned to her normal shape and ran to tell her father the good news.

Erysichthon Sells His Daughter Mestra, engraved by Johann Wilhelm Bauer for an edition of Ovid's *Metamorphoses* around 1639. *Metamorphoses* is a collection of myths that involve a character who changes shape—as Mestra does to escape those to whom Erysichthon sells her.

Minos Stands in Judgment in Dante's Inferno by Gustave Doré, engraved between 1861 and 1865. King Minos asked Poseidon for help, which the god granted. But when Minos went back on his word, Poseidon became angry and sought revenge.

Erysichthon, seeing an opportunity to make money, continued to sell Mestra. Each time he did so, Poseidon changed her into another form that enabled her to escape her new owner and return to her father. Finally, even this was not enough for Erysichthon. He turned on his own body and began eating his flesh until he died.

The tale of how the famous Minotaur—a human with a bull's head—came to be also features Poseidon. Minos (MY-nohs) was the king of the island of Crete, but his hold on the position was shaky. He prayed for Poseidon to give him a bull, which would show that he was favored by the gods and should be the rightful king. He vowed to sacrifice the animal in Poseidon's honor. Suddenly a magnificent white bull came charging out of the surf and onto the land.

It was the most superb animal that Minos had ever seen, and he felt he couldn't sacrifice it. He decided to use it for breeding stock and sacrifice another bull to Poseidon in its place.

The god was not pleased with this decision, so he made Minos' wife, Pasiphae, fall in love with the white bull. Day after day, Pasiphae could think of only the white bull. Finally she asked the master craftsman Daedalus (DAY-duh-lus) to help her. He built an artificial cow that Pasiphae could operate from the inside. She could approach the white bull without being noticed.

After spending time with the bull, Pasiphae became pregnant. Their baby was a monstrosity. He was human from his shoulders down, but he possessed the head and face of a bull. As soon as Minos saw the child he knew what had happened, and realized that this was Poseidon's revenge. He asked Daedalus to construct a labyrinth in which to imprison the creature, known as the Minotaur. The monster would live there, demanding human sacrifices, until the hero Theseus devised a plan to kill it.

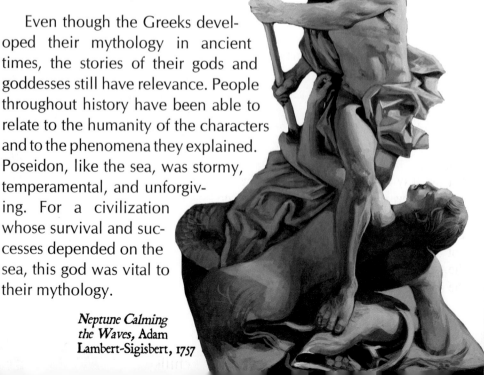

Even though the Greeks developed their mythology in ancient times, the stories of their gods and goddesses still have relevance. People throughout history have been able to relate to the humanity of the characters and to the phenomena they explained. Poseidon, like the sea, was stormy, temperamental, and unforgiving. For a civilization whose survival and successes depended on the sea, this god was vital to their mythology.

Neptune Calming the Waves, Adam Lambert-Sigisbert, 1757

The Minotaur

Theseus and the Minotaur in the Labyrinth, mosaic

The labyrinth Daedalus built to imprison the Minotaur had so many twists and turns that it was impossible to escape from it. Every nine years seven virgin females and seven other youths, all from Athens, were forced to enter the labyrinth as sacrifices for the Minotaur.

King Aegeus explained the sacrifices to Theseus when the hero came to Athens. Theseus decided that the terror must end, so he volunteered to go to Crete as one of the sacrifices and then kill the Minotaur. The ship on which the youths were taken to their doom had a black sail. Before it left Athens, Aegeus, the mortal father of Theseus, gave his son a white sail and told him to fly it on his return if he survived; that way the king would know from afar if Theseus had been victorious. When Theseus landed in Crete he fell in love with Minos' daughter Ariadne (ayr-ee-AD-nee). She said that she would help him defeat the

Dionysus meets Ariadne on Naxos

Minotaur if he took her back to Athens with him as his wife. Theseus agreed, so Ariadne went to Daedalus and found out the secret of the labyrinth.

Upon her return she gave Theseus a ball of thread. She told him to fasten it to the door when he first entered the labyrinth, then let it play out behind him as he moved through the maze. Theseus did so, and it worked perfectly. After he killed the Minotaur, he followed the string back out. He and Ariadne fled Crete. On the way home they stopped at the island of Naxos, where Athena told Theseus to abandon Ariadne. He sailed back to Athens alone.

Everything worked out all right for Ariadne, for she met the god Dionysus (dy-oh-NY-sus) on Naxos and married him. But Theseus forgot to raise the white sail on his return home. When King Aegeus saw the black sail, he hurled himself into the sea that now bears his name—the Aegean Sea.

Chapter 1. The Contest

1. Edith Hamilton, *Mythology* (New York: New American Library, 1989), p. 269.

2. Felix Guirand, *Greek Mythology* (London, England. Batchworth Press, 1963) p. 33.

3. Edith Hamilton, *Mythology* (New York: New American Library, 1989), p. 269.

4. Robert Graves, *The Greek Myths* (London, England: Penguin Books, 1992) p. 60.

Chapter 2. Poseidon's Family Tree

1. Felix Guirand. *Greek Mythology* (London, England. Batchworth Press, 1963) p. 71.

2. Edith Hamilton, *Mythology* (New York: New American Library, 1989), p. 29.

3. Guirand, p. 71.

4. Ibid.

5. Ibid.

6. Ibid., p. 72.

7. Ibid., p. 71.

8. Ibid.

9. Charles Seltman, *The Twelve Olympians* (New York: Thomas Y. Crowell, 1960), p. 143.

10. Ibid., p. 143.

11. Robert Graves, *The Greek Myths* (London, England: Penguin Books, 1992), p. 59.

12. David Kravitz, *Who's Who In Greek and Roman Mythology* (New York: Clarkson N. Potter, Inc., 1975), p. 210.

Chapter 3. Everyday Greek Life

1. Homer, *The Odyssey,* translated by Richmond Lattimore (New York: HarperPerennial, 1991), Book 4, lines 500–511.

2. H.D. Amos and A.G.P. Lang, *These Were the Greeks* (Chester Springs, Pennsylvania: Dufour Editions, Inc., 1982), p. 141.

3. Ibid., p. 142.

4. Ibid., p. 146.

5. Ibid., p. 155.

6. Ibid., p. 159.

7. Ibid.

Chapter 4. The Many Loves of Poseidon

1. Felix Guirand, *Greek Mythology* (London, England. Batchworth Press, 1963), p. 73.

2. Ovid, *Metamorphoses,* translated by Brookes More, Book, 4, lines 770–803; online at http://www.theoi.com/Text/OvidMetamorphoses4.html

3. Robert Graves, *The Greek Myths* (London, England: Penguin Books, 1992), p. 129.

4. Edith Hamilton, *Mythology* (New York: New American Library, 1989), p. 146.

5. Graves, p. 61.

6. Homer, *Odyssey,* translated by Richmond Lattimore (New York: HarperPerennial, 1991) Book 11, lines 238–254.

7. Apollodorus, *The Library,* translated by J. G. Frazer, volume I, 9.8–11; online at http://www.theoi.com/Text/Apollodorus1.html

Chapter 5. Tales of Poseidon

1. Homer, *Odyssey,* translated by Richmond Lattimore (New York: HarperPerennial, 1991) Book 9, lines 346–347.

2. Ibid, line 366.)Lattimore uses "Nobody," but modern children are more familiar with the "Noman" version.)

3. Ibid., line 408.

4. Ibid., lines 502–504.

5. Donald Richardson, *Great Zeus and All His Children* (Columbus, Ohio: Greyden Press, 1993) p. 266.

6. Edith Hamilton, *Mythology* (New York: New American Library, 1989), p. 285.

FURTHER READING

For Young Adults

Evslin, Bernard. *Heroes, Gods and Monsters of the Greek Myths*. New York: Dell Laurel-Leaf, 2005.

Ferguson, Diana. *Greek Myths & Legends*. New York: Sterling Publishers, 2000.

Hoena, B.A. *Poseidon*. Mankato, Minnesota: Capstone Press, 2004.

Osborne, Mary Pope. *The Land of the Dead*. New York: Hyperion Books for Children, 2002.

Spies, Karen Bornemann. *The Iliad and the Odyssey in Greek Mythology*. Berkeley Heights, New Jersey: Enslow, 2002.

Whiting, Jim. *Jason*. Hockessin, Delaware: Mitchell Lane Publishers, 2008.

Works Consulted

Amos, H.D., and A.G.P. Lang. *These Were the Greeks*. Chester Springs, Pennsylvania: Dufour Editions, Inc., 1982.

Apollodorus. *The Library*. Translated by J. G. Frazer. Online at
http://www.theoi.com/Text/Apollodorus1.html

Broneer, Oscar. "The Isthmian Games." *Proceedings of the International Olympic Academy*. http://www.ioa.leeds.ac.uk/1970s/70094.htm

Graves, Robert. *The Greek Myths*. London, England: Penguin Books, 1992.

Guirand, Felix. *Greek Mythology*. London, England. Batchworth Press, 1963.

Hamilton, Edith. *Mythology*. New York: New American Library, 1989.

Homer. *Odyssey*. Translated by Richmond Lattimore. New York: HarperPerennial, 1991.

Kravitz, David. *Who's Who In Greek and Roman Mythology*. New York: Clarkson N. Potter, Inc., 1975.

March, Jenny. *Dictionary of Classical Mythology*. New York: Sterling Publishing Co., 1998.

Osborn, Kevin, and Dana L. Burgess. *The Complete Idiot's Guide to Classical Mythology*. New York: Alpha Books, 1998.

Ovid. *Metamorphoses*. Translated by Brookes More. http://www.theoi.com/Text/OvidMetamorphoses1.html

Richardson, Donald. *Great Zeus and All His Children*. Columbus, Ohio: Greyden Press, 1993.

Seltman, Charles. *The Twelve Olympians*. New York: Thomas Y. Crowell, 1960.

Stapleton, Michael. *The Illustrated Dictionary of Greek and Roman Mythology*. New York: Peter Bedrick Books, 1986.

On the Internet

Encyclopedia Mythica: Greek mythology
http://www.pantheon.org/areas/mythology/europe/greek/

Greek Mythology
http://www.greekmythology.com

Greek Mythology
http://www.mythweb.com/

The Immortals: Greek Mythology
http://messagenet.com/myths/chart.html

commotion (kuh-MOH-shun)—Noisy disturbance.

Cyclops (SY-klops)—A race of giants with one huge eye in the center of their forehead. The plural of *Cyclops* is *Clyclopes* (sy-KLOH-peez).

deity (DEE-uh-tee)—A god or goddess.

devise (dee-VYZ)—To plan.

drab—Dull.

haggard (HAG-urd)—Having an exhausted appearance.

hierarchy (HY-er-ar-kee)—Any system that ranks one above the other.

intervene (in-ter-VEEN)—To come between.

intricate (IN-trih-kit)—Complicated.

labyrinth (LAA-buh-rinth)—A maze.

personification (per-sah-nih-fih-KAY-shun)—Giving human qualities to something that is not human.

relevant (REH-luh-vunt)—Connected to the matter at hand.

sickle (SIH-kul)—A curved blade used for cutting grain, grass, etc.

smug—Confident of one's own ability.

solemn (SOL-um)—Very serious.

subordinate (sub-OR-dih-nit)—Of a lower order or rank.

suitor (SOO-tor)—A man who courts a woman.

tryst (TRIST)—An appointment to meet at a certain time or place.

wake (WAYK)—The track of waves left by a ship.